The Usborne
STORY
OF
MUSIC

Simon Mundy

Illustrated by Joseph McEwan

Designed by Graham Round and Kim Blundell

Edited by Robyn Gee

Contents

Consultant Editor: Dr Anne Millard

First published in 1980 by Usborne Publishing Ltd
Usborne House, 83-85 Saffron Hill, London EC1N 8RT
Copyright © 1980 Usborne Publishing Ltd

Printed in Belgium

Music in the Ancient World

The story of music goes back to prehistoric times and we can only guess at how it began. Even before people started making instruments, they made music, probably by singing, clapping or hitting things. Most experts agree that people first made music for magical or religious reasons, and it has had an important place in religion ever since. By the time the first great civilisations of the Ancient World had emerged, a great variety of musical instruments were already in use.

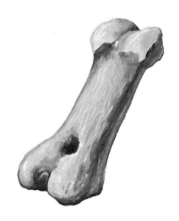

This is a whistle made in France about 20,000 years ago, from a piece of reindeer horn. Perhaps it was used to copy bird-songs.

1 Egyptian musicians

In Egypt many of the royal musicians were women and they were often buried near the royal tombs. Music was involved in every part of life. Dancers and flute players accompanied work in the fields and the treading of the grapes. Here you can see the sort of instruments the Egyptians played.

Most of the evidence for musical activity in the Ancient World comes from pictures. This one dates from about 4000 years ago and shows musicians in the ancient country of Sumer.

Assyrian captives

In most ancient civilisations, musicians were thought very important, second only to the kings and priests. This was especially true in Assyria. When their army captured an enemy city, they always spared the lives of the musicians.

Music was also important in temple ceremonies. Here flutes and sistra (a kind of rattle) are being played. Silver and bronze instruments, like trumpets, were used mainly by the army.

Greek music

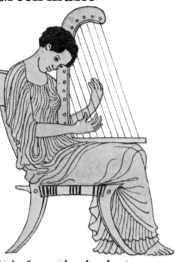

It is from the Ancient Greeks that we get the word "music". They called it *mousike*, after the nine muses, goddesses of inspiration.

The Greeks attached great importance to music. Each year in Athens a singing competition was held. Every district formed a choir and sang a *dythyramb*, which was a kind of hymn. People wore special costumes and there was dancing as well. The

Choir singing a dythyramb.

Greeks also used songs in their plays. These were performed at festivals in honour of the god Dionysius.

This vase painting of a music lesson shows some of the instruments used by the Greeks. Most of these came from the Middle East. The main ones were the harp, or lyre, which they called a kithara, and a reed pipe, called an aulos.

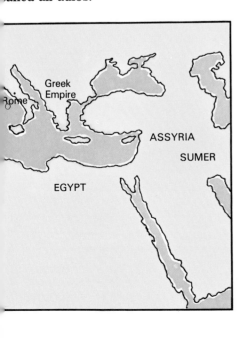

Rome
Greek Empire
ASSYRIA
SUMER
EGYPT

Music in the Roman Empire

Trumpet

Cymbals

In Rome, as in Greece, plays were accompanied by music and so were the gladiator fights. Trumpets and cymbals were used, as shown here, and also pipes, drums and organs.

Jugglers and acrobats performed in the city streets with people playing pipes and tambourines.

Kithara

Wealthy people held concerts in their villas. These musicians are playing pipes and a Roman version of the kithara.

Singers gave big public concerts and were often very well paid. The Emperor Nero, who sang and played the kithara, gave a concert at the theatre in Pompeii in AD65. The next year he toured Greece as a singer. Here he is giving a concert.

Music of the Middle East

The music of the Middle East developed from the traditions and instruments of the ancient civilisations of the area, and so sounds very different from that of Europe. As in Africa and the Far East, the music is accompanied by an instrument which provides the rhythm. The tune is often made up of five basic notes and the sound is varied by putting lots of extra notes between the main ones, so the music sounds as if it is sliding about the scale.

Music has never played a very important part in the Muslim religion, which is followed all over the Middle East, as it was banned by the prophet Muhammad, who founded the religion. However from about the 8th century, music played a major part in life at the courts and palaces of rulers, like the Sultan of Baghdad, shown here.

Taar
Kovitra
Kemendjah
Tunbur
Kanoun

The music of the Arab peoples today sounds very much as it always has done. The tune is provided by a wind instrument or a singer, while the rhythm is played by the drums. There is usually a rebab, an ud or a tunbur accompanying them as well. Although there are often several players, there are no orchestras in the western sense.

SPAIN
MIDDLE EAST
NORTH AFRICA
AFRICA

1 The influence of Arab music in Europe

Ud
Rebab

Arab music has had a great influence on European music. After the Crusades, minstrels brought back instruments they had heard, such as the ud and rebab, which became called the lute and rebec.

2

Between the 8th and 15th centuries, Arabs from North Africa invaded and occupied large parts of Spain. At Cordova they founded a school of music and now many Spanish dances have Arab sounds in them.

3

Instruments used in Turkish military bands were brought back from the Middle East during the Crusades. Some of these, such as the shawm, became popular in European bands.

4

African Music

In African villages, music and dancing are part of everyone's life. Every important occasion, such as the birth of a baby, a marriage or a burial, has special music and dancing to go with it.

African music is not written down, it is memorized and passed down from one generation to the next. We only know about the music of the past from clues like this rock painting found in the Sahara Desert.

The people of the kingdom of Benin, in West Africa, left records of the past in the form of bronze plaques. Many of these show musicians, like this drummer, who evidently played an important part in life there.

Instrument making

Traditional instruments in Africa are made from materials which can be found around the village. Drums are made from hollowed logs with animal skins as drum heads. Gourds are used for xylophones and rattles.

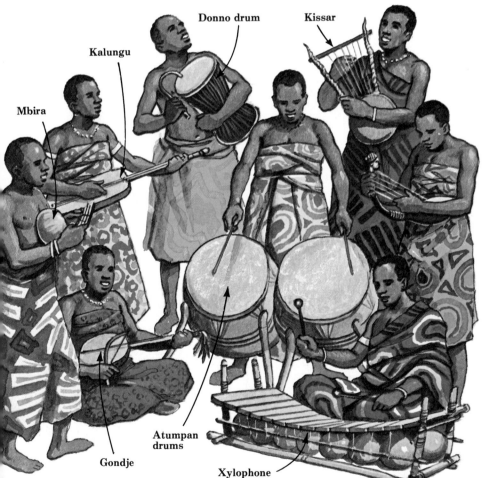

Mbira
Kalungu
Donno drum
Kissar
Atumpan drums
Gondje
Xylophone

Talking drums

In many African languages words can change their meaning according to how high or low you say them. A drummer can imitate the way Africans speak by altering the tightness of the skin on the drum and by hitting it in different places.

African musicians use a great variety of instruments, especially percussion instruments (ones you hit). The donno drum from West Africa looks like an hour-glass and the atumpan drums are rather like kettledrums. The stringed instruments include a sort of guitar called a kalungu, a harp very similar to the ones played in the ancient world and a lyre called a kissar.

Music in the East

The main forms of Indian music can be traced back nearly 2,000 years, to the first chanting of hymns in the Hindu temples. The other countries of Asia and the Far East have a musical history which is just as ancient.

India has a tradition of both folk and classical music. Until quite recently, Indian classical music was played mostly in the palaces of the Indian princes, but now Indian musicians give recitals all over the world.

India

The rules of Indian music are passed down by word of mouth from a *guru* (teacher) to his pupil over many years of study. Its basis is the art of improvisation (making up the music as you go along). The composer provides a set of notes called the *rag* (tune or melody), and the rhythm, called the *tala*. It is then up to the musician to invent the rest of the music around this basic framework provided by the composer.

Vichitra veena · Mirdang · Sarod · Sitar · Tambura · Sarangi · Tabla

Singers and flute players are both popular in India, but stringed instruments, such as the sitar, are more commonly heard. Indian musicians use many more notes than western musicians. To people not used to eastern music, they often sound like western notes played slightly out of tune.

Indonesia

Saron · Gender · Bonang

In Indonesia an orchestra is called a *gamelan*. It often includes singers and colourfully dressed dancers. The word *gamel* means a hammer, and so the *gamelan* is mainly made up of instruments that are hit. The most popular are the gender, the saron (a sort of xylophone), and the bonang (a set of knobbed gongs played with padded sticks). A *gamelan* varies in size, from a few performers, to over 70.

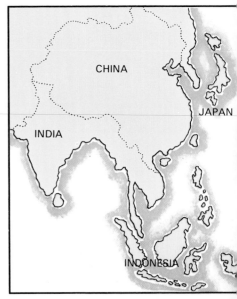

CHINA · JAPAN · INDIA · INDONESIA

China

P'ip'a

Hu ch'in

Very little Chinese music is heard outside China, with the exception of Chinese opera. It can be traced back to the court poetry and folk theatres of at least 1,000 years ago. It has dancing, mime and exotic costumes as well as singing. There are two sets of instruments which accompany the action and singing. The first, for battles and grand entrances, has cymbals, drums, gongs and wind instruments. The second, for quieter scenes, has a small drum, the hu ch'in, which is played with a bow, and the p'ip'a, which is plucked.

Japan

Biwa

Shamisen

The koto

One of the most popular types of Japanese music is the music of the Kabuki Theatre. The players sit on the stage and behind the scenery. They have, among other instruments, the biwa and the shamisen, both kinds of Japanese lutes. The actors wear beautiful costumes. They are all men, even those who are playing women's roles.

One of the most beautiful-sounding of Japanese instruments is the koto. It is tuned by moving bridges under the strings, which are plucked with picks fastened onto the fingers.

The Middle Ages

When the Roman Empire finally collapsed in the 7th century AD, many of the arts that had developed in the Ancient World died with it. But music was kept alive in the churches and monasteries. There were minstrels too, who continued the traditions of the musicians, acrobats and jugglers of the Roman streets. Some wandered from town to town, others were employed by nobles. It was during this period that the present system of writing down music began to be developed.

Much of the church music was sung on its own in a form called plainchant or plainsong. The choir sung a simple tune in unison (everyone singing the same note at the same time). This is often called Gregorian chant, because many of the rules for its use were laid down when Gregory the Great was Pope (AD590/604). Some churches had organs but they were not used much.

When Charlemagne (AD742/815) was crowned as the first Holy Roman Emperor, he invited singers to his court at Aix-la-Chapelle. There composers began to set the words of the Roman poets to music.

Some of these Latin poems were written down by monks with the music to which they were sung. These collections were kept in the monastery libraries.

Writing music down

The system of writing music down developed slowly over a long period of time. In the Middle Ages written music looked very different from the way it does now.

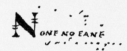

By about the 7th century there was a system that used marks above the words to be sung. The marks were called neumes and they showed the singer roughly how the music went but not the exact pitch and length of the notes.

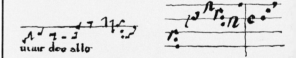

Then people started drawing a line to represent one particular note. Neumes above the line were higher notes, neumes below the line were lower notes. Soon more lines were added. Each line and space stood for a different note. These lines are called a stave or staff.

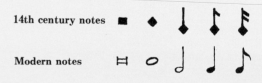

14th century notes			
Modern notes			

Gradually, as music became more complicated, a system which could show the length of a note was needed, and so shapes were introduced.

Musical instruments of the Middle Ages

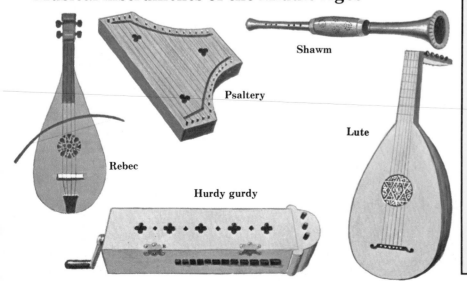

Shawm

Psaltery

Rebec

Hurdy gurdy

Lute

Minstrels

Minstrels were the people who sang, played and wrote the non-religious music of the Middle Ages. There were several types of minstrel. Travelling musicians, who often included jugglers and acrobats in their troupes, were called *jongleurs* in France, and gleemen in England.

In France, where there was a long period of peace in the 11th and 12th centuries, noblemen concentrated on writing music and poetry. In southern France they became known as troubadours, in the north as *trouvères*. One of their favourite subjects was the love of gallant knights for beautiful ladies.

Many of these noble poet-musicians were knights who had taken part in the Crusades against the Muslim Turks. One of the most famous was Richard the Lionheart, King of England. The musicians among the Crusaders brought back many musical ideas and instruments from the Arab world.

In Germany the troubadours were called *minnesingers,* which means "singers of love". As the centuries went by their place was taken by the mastersingers, who were usually townspeople. Their guilds held competitions for the best songs. Here you can see a mastersinger, accompanied by musicians.

The "new art"

From about 1300 onwards, some composers started to write much more complicated music. They used more varied rhythms and several lines of melody sung at the same time. This style became known as Ars Nova, which means "new art" in Latin. The most famous centre of this type of music was in Paris, where the great cathedral of Notre-Dame (shown above) was being built.

Some of the composers working at this time are among the first to be remembered by name. Two of the most famous composers of this type of music were Guillaume de Machaut, a French priest, and Francesco Landini, a blind organist from Florence in Italy. Both men were poets as well as musicians, and both composed non-religious songs as well as music to be sung at church services.

Landini

Machaut

Renaissance Music

During the 15th century great changes were taking place in Europe, especially in the way people thought about the world they lived in. New ideas and attitudes affected every area of life—politics, religion, science and, above all, the arts. This period of time is known as the Renaissance.

In music there were several important changes. Church music was still very important but many composers now worked at the courts of wealthy rulers and composed non-religious music as well. People also started to compose music for instruments as well as for voices. But the greatest music of the period was still that written for voices and this vocal music became far more complicated than ever before.

This banquet is at the Duke of Burgundy's court. He ruled an independent province in eastern France. In the 15th century, he employed many of the best musicians in Europe.

The court of the Popes in Rome was another important centre for musicians. Composers, such as Josquin des Près and Giovanni Palestrina, both worked there.

The rulers of England were keen patrons of musicians. King Henry VIII was himself a good composer and musician. He wrote church music, songs and music for dances, like the one above. The reign of his daughter, Queen Elizabeth I, is often thought of as the greatest age of English music, as it produced many of England's best known composers.

Church music

Much of the best music of this time was written for the Church. After the Reformation Protestants started writing music to be sung by the whole congregation, not just by the choir. They also started writing the words in the language of their own country, rather than in Latin. Some musicians continued to write for the Roman Catholic Church.

During the Renaissance madrigals became very popular. These are songs (usually about love) for small groups of voices without any instruments to accompany them.

Madrigals originated in Italy and were performed at all sorts of occasions, especially feasts. This one was to celebrate the wedding of one of the Medici family of Florence.

Some famous Renaissance composers

Here are a few of the composers who wrote some of the best music of the Renaissance. Most of them travelled widely in Europe and composed both Church music and non-religious music.

Josquin des Près came from the Netherlands and worked at several courts in France and Italy.

Roland de Lassus came from the Netherlands. He wrote nearly 1,000 works including many Italian madrigals.

The Italian, Giovanni Palestrina, wrote most of his music for the churches of Rome.

Guillaume Dufay came from the Netherlands but worked in France, Italy and Burgundy, composing both church music and songs.

Jean de Ockeghem, also from the Netherlands, was a pupil of Dufay. He worked mainly at the French court.

William Byrd was an Englishman. He was organist at the Chapel Royal and composed mainly church music.

Thomas Tallis was English. He worked with Byrd at the Chapel Royal and shared with him the monopoly of printing music.

Renaissance instruments

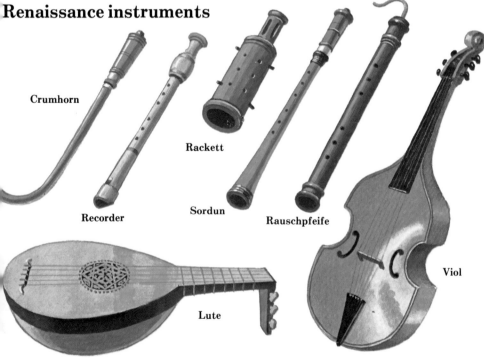

Crumhorn

Recorder

Rackett

Sordun

Rauschpfeife

Viol

Lute

In the Renaissance musical instruments began to be grouped together in sets of four or more. Each instrument in the set covered a different range of notes. If the set consisted of different sizes of the same type of instrument, it was called a consort. Viols, recorders, shawms and racketts all came in different sizes, which were played together as consorts.

Music to listen to

Dunstable (died AD1453)
Ave Marie Stella (song)

Machaut (AD1300/1377)
Notre Dame Mass

Henry VIII (AD1491/1547)
Passtime with good company (madrigal)

Tallis (AD1505/1585)
Spem in Alium (choral work)

Palestrina (AD1525/1594)
Missa Brevis in 4 parts (church music)

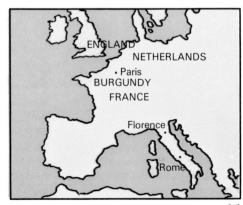

Early Opera and Ballet

In the 17th century, the period called Baroque, music developed into forms which can be more easily recognized today. The way music was printed began to change. The violin became an important instrument for the first time, and keyboard instruments, such as the harpsichord, were used more than ever before. But the furthest reaching new idea of all was opera. One of the first composers of opera was Claudio Monteverdi, whose opera *Orpheo* was first performed in 1607.

Venice was an important centre of music at this time. The world's first public opera house opened there in 1637. Many of the great Italian composers worked at St Mark's Cathedral, shown above.

Opera in Italy

The idea for opera came from a group of poets and composers who met in Florence in the 1590s. They thought that the kind of music used in plays at that time was too complicated and interfered with the stories. So they imagined what a Greek play would have been like, with clear, simple music for the singer and a very simpl accompaniment. This new style they called recitative. Above you can see a scene from an early opera.

1 England

One of the most famous English composers of this time was John Dowland. He wrote many songs for the lute, which was the most popular instrument of this period.

Lute songs were also used a lot in the theatres, like the Globe in London, where Shakespeare's plays were performed. One of the best composers of these songs was called Robert Johnson.

Johnson also wrote music for the court masques of James I and Charles I. These were very expensive entertainments with music, dancing and beautiful moving scenery.

The first English opera wa performed in 1656, when Oliver Cromwell ruled the country. It was called *The Siege of Rhodes* and this is a design for scenery used in the original performance.

1 The French court

The conductor of Louis XIV's orchestra was Jean Baptiste Lully, who also wrote and performed in many ballets. He died of a poisonous leg after hitting himself with his conducting stick.

The French court was the most magnificent in Europe. King Louis XIII and his son, Louis XIV were both very musical and made sure that they hired all the best musicians and artists. Louis XIV had an orchestra of 24 violins, which was later copied by Charles II in England. He also studied the guitar and the harpsichord and put on ballets at his palace at Versailles, in which he often appeared himself.

Music to listen to

Purcell (AD1659/1695)
Dido and Aeneas (opera)
Ode to St Cecilia
Chaconny in G for strings

Monteverdi (AD1567/1633)
Orpeo (opera)
Vespers of 1610 (church music)

Dowland (AD1563/1626)
Sorrow Stay (song)
Queen Elizabeth's Galliard (lute music)

Johnson (AD1583/1633)
Full Fathom Five (song from the Tempest)

Lully (AD1632/1687)
Grand Divertissements Royal de Versailles

The violin family

Violin

Viola

Cello

Violins were originally instruments for dancing to. In the 17th century, with violas and cellos, they gradually replaced the viol family in serious music.

The harpsichord

Strings
(These are plucked by quills)

Keyboard

From the 16th to the 18th centuries the harpsichord was the most important keyboard instrument.

Baroque Music

By 1700, several distinct instrumental forms (ways in which the music is arranged and presented) had developed. In the first half of the 18th century these were developed still further. Some of the composers of this period are considered to be among the greatest of any age.

Although music was still strongly associated with the church, music for entertainment was becoming more important, and this period saw the beginning of public concerts.

Antonio Vivaldi lived in Venice, where he was well-known as a violinist. He was a priest, and because of his vivid red hair he became known as "the red priest".

He taught for most of his life at a girls' school, the Pieta. Here his pupils are giving a concert. As well as operas and church music, Vivaldi wrote over 600 concertos.

Pleasure gardens

Throughout the 17th and 18th centuries, there were public performances of music in the various London Pleasure Gardens, such as Vauxhall and Ranelagh.

The idea of a concert, in the sense of a public performance at which an audience pays for the right of admittance, began towards the end of the 17th century.

The concerto

The word "concerto" comes from the Italian word meaning "concert" or "playing together". In the late 17th and early 18th century it was used to describe a piece of music to be played by a small group of solo instruments and an orchestra. A piece like this was called a concerto grosso. Vivaldi, Handel and Bach all composed this type of concerto.

Dance music

Dances were the first kind of music composed only for instruments. In the 17th century, they began to be written together in sets or "suites". The Frenchman, Jean Philippe Rameau, wrote many such dances, both for groups of instruments as part of his ballets, and for the harpsichord. François Couperin also wrote suites for the harpsichord.

Famous violin makers

At this time there were three famous families of violin makers, all working in the Italian town of Cremona. They were the Amati, the Guarneri and the Stradivari. Instruments made in the workshops of these families are very valuable now, especially those of Antonio Stradivari, who is considered one of the greatest instrument makers of all time.

1 Bach

Johann Sebastian Bach came from a family of musicians and grew up with music all around him. He had 20 children of his own, many of whom went into the music profession.

2

Bach was a very great organist. This is the organ of the church at Arnstadt, which he played when he was organist there. He composed a lot of church music—cantatas, oratorios and passions.

3

Bach also worked at the courts of Weimar, and of Cöthen, where he directed all the prince's singers and musicians. He composed a great deal of chamber music—concertos and suites—to be played at court.

1 Handel

George Frederic Handel was born in Saxony, in Germany. From there he moved to Italy, where he learnt the latest fashions in music. In 1711 he went to London and spent most of the rest of his life in England.

2

Handel wrote many operas. Although his first ones were a success, opera began to lose popularity in England and he found it more and more difficult to find money with which to finance them. So Handel started writing oratorios, such as The Messiah, instead. An oratorio is rather like an opera with a religious theme. It is performed by an orchestra, a chorus and soloists, but without any costumes or action.

3

Handel was a great favourite, both of King George II and his father, King George I. He wrote a lot of music for royal occasions, such as the coronation of George II. George I liked to travel on the River Thames, with boatloads of courtiers in a great procession of barges, and have music playing as he was rowed along. Handel wrote many pieces for this and gathered them together to form *The Water Music.*

Music to listen to

J.S.Bach (AD1685/1750)
The Brandenburg Concertos Nos. 1–6.
Magnificat in D major. (church music)
Jesu, Joy of Man's Desiring.
Concerto for 2 Violins and strings in D

J.C.Bach (AD1735/1782)
Symphonies Op.18., Nos. 1–6.

Handel (AD1685/1759)
The Messiah (Oratorio)
The Water Music
Music for the Royal Fireworks

Vivaldi (AD1685/1759)
Concertos Op.8., 1–4, 'The Four Seasons',
Gloria in D major (church music)

Classical Music

Although people often call all serious music "classical", the Classical period really refers to the second half of the 18th century. It was then that many of the standard forms of music, such as the symphony, sonata and concerto, were developed. This development can best be seen in the work of Mozart and Haydn.

With the beginning of the 19th century, we move out of the Classical and into the Romantic Age, when musicians extended and further developed the Classical forms.

At this time Vienna was the most important centre of music and most of the famous composers of this period lived or worked there at least for a time.

Music to listen to

Haydn (AD1732/1809)
Symphony No. 100., "The Military"
The Nelson Mass (church music)
The Creation (oratorio)

Mozart (AD1756/1791)
The Magic Flute (opera)
Piano Concerto No. 20 in D minor
Serenade in G., "Eine Kleine Nachtmusik"

Beethoven (AD1770/1827)
Piano Concerto No. 5., "The Emperor"
Symphony No. 9., "The Choral"
String Quartets Nos. 7 & 8.,
"The Rasumovsky"

Schubert (AD1798/1828)
Symphony No. 9., "The Great C Major"
The Trout Quintet
Die Schone Mullerin (song cycle)

1 Haydn

For most of his life, Franz Joseph Haydn worked for Prince Esterhazy in Hungary (then part of the Austrian Empire), where he composed a new work nearly every week.

Violins   Viola   Cello

Altogether Haydn wrote 104 symphonies, as well as church masses and music for string quartets (above). A quartet is made up of two violins, a viola and a cello. It is an important

form of chamber music—music originally designed to be played at home. Quartets were very rarely played in public until the middle of the 19th century.

1 Mozart

Wolfgang Amadeus Mozart was only six when he gave his first concert and played for the Emperor, Francis I, in Vienna. At nine, he wrote his first symphony. Here he is with his father and sister.

Writing music was never difficult for Mozart. Although he was only 35 when he died, he still managed to write 41 symphonies and 27 piano concertos, as well as some of the world's most famous operas.

Mozart set some of his operas in his own time, breaking away from the traditional setting of Ancient Greece or Rome. *The Marriage of Figaro*, put on in 1786, was thought daring, as it criticized noblemen.

1 Beethoven

Ludwig van Beethoven was among the first of the Romantic composers. He was also a great pianist and played all five of his piano concertos at their first performances.

2

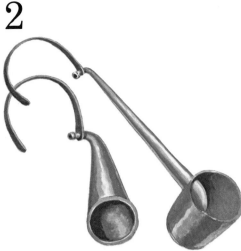

In his 30s Beethoven began to go deaf, but he went on composing until his death about 20 years later. Here are some of the ear trumpets he used to help him hear.

3

Beethoven wrote nine symphonies. In his ninth he included singers and a chorus in the last movement. Before this symphonies had only used the instruments of the orchestra.

The Classical symphony

The word "symphony" means "sounding together" and was first used in the 17th century to describe almost any kind of music for instruments, as opposed to music for voices. By the 18th century "symphony" meant a large scale work for an orchestra and by the end of the century what is known as the "Classical symphony" had appeared.

A Classical symphony usually has four "movements" or sections:
1. A fairly fast, lively movement.
2. A slow movement.
3. A minuet and trio.
4. A fast, cheerful movement.

The Classical concerto

The Classical concerto grew out of the concerto grosso* of the first half of the 18th century. It has a single soloist (instead of a group of soloists, as the concerto grosso had) and consists of three movements:
1. A serious movement. This begins with the orchestra playing alone; the soloist joins in a bit later.
2. A slower movement.
3. A fast movement.

Often a "cadenza" is included towards the end of the first, or last movement, or in both. This is played by the soloist alone, unaccompanied by the orchestra.

The Classical sonata

Sonata originally referred to any piece of music that was played rather than sung. During the 17th and early 18th centuries it was used to describe various kinds of musical composition. By the middle of the 18th century the Classical sonata had emerged.

Classical sonatas are either for a single keyboard instrument, or for a keyboard instrument and one other instrument. They usually have four movements arranged as follows:
1. A long, quick movement.
2. A slow movement.
3. A minuet and trio.
4. A quick and lively movement.

Schubert

Franz Schubert was a young contemporary of Beethoven, from Vienna. Besides symphonies he wrote many songs, or *lieder,* as they are called in German. Here he is playing one of his songs to his friends.

Pianos

Square piano (rarely seen nowadays)

Upright piano (made for playing at home)

Grand piano (usually found in concert halls)

The real name for a piano is a pianoforte, which means "soft-loud" in Italian. It was invented in 1710 in Italy, and became very popular in the Classical period. The difference between pianos and earlier keyboard instruments is that the strings are hit with hammers, instead of being plucked. The harder you strike the keys the louder the notes sound.

*See page 14

The Orchestra

Orchestras developed gradually out of the court bands of the 17th century. Instruments were constantly being improved and new ones added. By about 1830 the modern orchestra was more or less complete. There are usually between 70 and 100 musicians, depending on the music to be played, and there are sometimes soloists and a chorus as well.

Here you can see the main instruments and the way they are usually arranged in the orchestra.

Brass

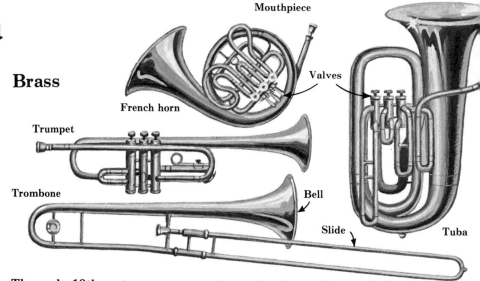

The early 19th century was a great period of mechanical invention, in musical instruments, as in other areas. The greatest improvement in brass instruments was the invention of the valve. Valves, when pressed by the players fingers, bring into use extra lengths of tubing, as well as the main tube, making it possible to play all the notes of the scale. The longer the tube of a brass instrument is, the lower the notes it can play.

Woodwind

Wind instruments, like those above, became gradually easier to play throughout the 18th and 19th centuries. Keys (levers to open and close the holes mechanically) were added so that players could find the notes much faster and more accurately.

Percussion

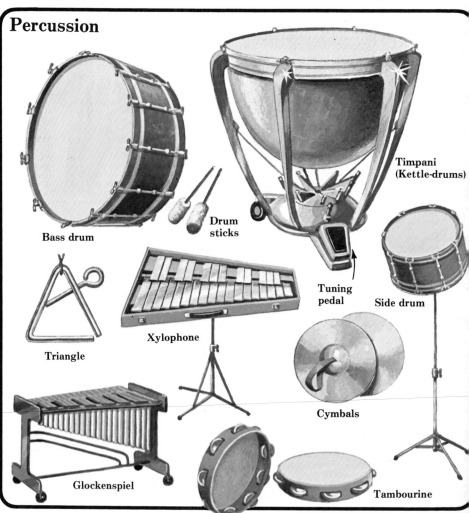

The percussion section of an orchestra can include any instrument which produces a sound when you hit it. In the Classical and early Romantic periods composers rarely used more than the timpani. It was not until the end of the 19th century that percussion became used on any large scale. In the 20th century it has become more and more important and is now often one of the largest sections.

For more information see page 13.

Strings

Violin
Viola
Cello
Double bass

These are the instruments of the string section, drawn to scale. For more information see page 13.

Percussion

Brass

Woodwind

Violas

2nd violins

Harp   1st violins   Conductor   Cellos   Double basses

This picture shows a typical seating plan for a standard orchestra. The different families of instruments—strings, woodwind, brass and percussion—are grouped together. This basic arrangement has existed since the 19th century. Some conductors put the second violins where the cellos are in this picture. If there is a solo part the soloist is put on the left of the conductor.

Concert halls

The first concert halls were built towards the end of the 18th century. Now most big cities have one and many of them have seating for over 3,000 people.

1 The conductor

The conductor was originally a leading member of the orchestra, who used a violin bow, a roll of music or conducted from a keyboard instrument to keep the orchestra in time.

2

Now a conductor uses a finely balanced stick called a baton. He has to decide how fast the music should go and how loud or soft each part should be played.

The Romantics

The 19th century Romantic movement influenced all the arts. In music, composers now wanted to express their feelings and emotions. Beethoven and Schubert led the movement out of the Classical period and into the Romantic. This movement was carried further by the composers on these two pages. Paris and Vienna were Europe's main centres of music at this time. Public concerts became more popular, especially those with music for piano or orchestra.

Two of the most famous musicians of this period were Frederic Chopin, who was Polish, and Franz Liszt, a Hungarian. Both were brilliant pianists and composers of piano music, and both spent much of their lives in Paris. Liszt developed the "symphonic poem", a one-movement piece of music for orchestra, which tells a story. Chopin based much of his music on dances, such as the mazurka, the waltz and the polka.

Programme music

Programme music is any piece of music which tells a story or describes a scene, explained in a written programme. Below you can see four scenes from the story described by the *Symphonie Fantastique*, written by Hector Berlioz.

Berlioz falls in love with a woman. Everywhere he goes her face appears to him. Here he is at a ball, dreaming about her.

Even in the quiet countryside he cannot stop thinking about her, fearing that she is deceiving him.

He tries to kill himself by taking opium. He dreams he has murdered her and is watching his own execution.

In his dream, ghosts, sorcerers and monsters, joined by his beloved, surround him for the funeral.

This is Robert Schumann with his wife, Clara. Schumann was a composer of Romantic piano music. He also wrote songs and symphonies and was a music critic and journalist. Clara was one of the best pianists of her day. In his early 30s, Schumann began to go mad, and he died when still quite young.

The German, Felix Mendelssohn, was one of the most popular and successful composers of the 19th century. He was also famous as a conductor.

Mendelssohn was especially popular in England, where he was a great favourite of Queen Victoria. Here he is being presented to her.

The Viennese court

Johannes Brahms came from northern Germany, but lived in Vienna for the later part of his life. His music continued and developed the style established by Beethoven.

Anton Bruckner settled in Vienna in 1868 and was appointed court organist. He was a very religious man and wrote much music for use in church, as well as nine symphonies.

In the 19th century, Vienna was the capital city of the great Austro-Hungarian Empire, and the Viennese court was the most glittering in the world. It was a very lively place, where people loved to give dances and parties, each more spectacular than the last. For this they needed music. The favourite dances were the polka and, above all, the waltz. There were many composers writing these, but the most famous were a father and son, both called Johann Strauss.

Music to listen to

Chopin (AD1810/1849)
Piano Concerto No. 1
Sonata in B flat

Berlioz (AD1803/1869)
Le Corsaire (overture)
Harold in Italy (symphony)

Schumann (AD1810/1856)
Piano Concerto in A minor
Symphony No. 3, "The Rhenish"
Carnaval (for piano)

Mendelssohn (AD1809/1847)
The Hebrides Overture, "Fingal's Cave"
Music to 'A Midsummer Night's Dream'

Liszt (AD1811/1886)
Mazeppa (tone poem)
Mephisto Waltz No. 1

Tchaikovsky

Peter Ilyich Tchaikovsky was one of the first Russian composers to become internationally famous and his music has remained very popular. He wrote symphonies, concertos, operas and three famous ballets. Above is a scene from his ballet *Swan Lake*.

The Austrian composer, Gustav Mahler, also wrote nine symphonies. They need huge orchestras to play them and sometimes a big choir as well. He was a very talented conductor.

Opera

Almost all the most popular operas in the world today, apart from those of Mozart, were written during the last two centuries. In the 19th century operas became full of exciting action, spectacular costumes and scenery and flamboyant music. Operas of this period are often referred to as Grand Opera. During this time many people began to regard opera as the best way of uniting all the arts. Composers like Wagner and Verdi, and, in the 20th century, Britten and Janáček, saw opera as the most important part of their work. Until about 1850 almost all opera was in Italian, but from then on composers usually wrote the words in their own language.

1

Jenny Lind

Luigi Lablanche

In Italy, the music and singing mattered more than the story of an opera. Leading opera singers became very famous and were often angry if they were not given parts that allowed them to show off their voices. As a result composers wrote in a style known as *bel canto,* which means "beautiful singing". Above are two famous singers of the 19th century.

1 Richard Wagner

2

The German composer, Richard Wagner, believed that the story and the way it was told were as important in opera as the music. He thought that opera could be the greatest form of artistic expression, but felt that there were no opera houses which could stage his operas as he wanted them. With the help of King Ludwig II of Bavaria (shown above), he raised enough money to

3

4

have one built to his own design. It is the opera house at Bayreuth in Germany. Every year a festival of Wagner's work is held there. His greatest work was a series of four operas, based on stories from German myths, called *The Ring of the Nibelungs,* which was first performed in 1876. It lasts nearly 20 hours and took him 20 years to write.

2

3

Guiseppe Verdi was the most important composer of 19th century Italian opera. He continued the *bel canto* tradition, with dramatic stories, and tunes which were easy to remember. Verdi wrote 19 operas altogether. They cover a wide range of subjects. The scene above is from *Rigoletto,* which tells the tragic story of a hunchbacked court jester.

4

Giacomo Puccini followed in the tradition of Verdi, and after Verdi's death in 1901, Puccini became the leading Italian composer of opera. This scene is from *Madame Butterfly,* which is about a Japanese girl and an American sailor. This, and another of Puccini's operas, *La Bohème,* are two of the most popular of all operas because of their sad stories and flowing tunes.

1 20th century opera

Richard Strauss was a great admirer of Wagner. He too composed complex operas which need large orchestras. They vary from the lurid *Salome* (above) to the romantic *Der Rosenkavalier* (Cavalier of the Rose).

Leos Janáček, who was a Czech, was one of the most inventive composers of opera. This scene is from *The Cunning Little Vixen*, about a fox. Some of his other works, like *Jenufa*, are about ordinary village people.

Another classic of this century is *Wozzeck*, by Alban Berg. It is about a soldier in the Austrian army. It uses *sprechgesang* (speech-song), a half-speaking, half-singing style, developed by Arnold Schönberg.

Opera houses

The earliest opera houses were built in the 17th century, in big European cities like Venice, London, Paris, Rome and Berlin. In the 18th century many more were built. In Italy and Germany nearly every large town had its own opera house.

In the 19th century composers began writing for much larger orchestras. Bigger theatres were needed, and it was then that many of the world's greatest opera houses were built.

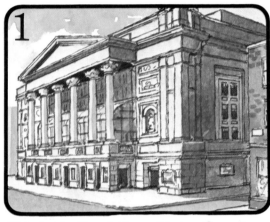

This is the Royal Opera House, Covent Garden, London. It was built in 1858. It is the third opera house to be built on this site. The two previous ones were destroyed by fire.

This is the inside of Milan's famous opera house, La Scala. The first performances of many of the great Italian operas, by composers like Verdi and Puccini, were staged here.

The Vienna State Opera first opened in 1869, but was completely rebuilt after being destroyed during World War II. In 1883 it became the first theatre to install electric lights.

The Sydney Opera House, which opened in 1973, is one of the few great opera houses built in the 20th century. It was designed by a Danish architect called Joern Utzon.

Music to listen to

Rossini (AD1792/1868)
The Barber of Seville
Cinderella

Verdi (AD1813/1901)
Aida
La Traviata

Wagner (AD1813/1883)
The Flying Dutchman
The Mastersingers of Nuremberg

Puccini (AD1858/1924)
Tosca
Turandot

Richard Strauss (AD1864/1949)
Arabella

National Music

In the middle of the 19th century there was much political unrest in Europe. Countries like Germany and Italy struggled to become unified nations, instead of collections of independent states. Many of the smaller countries struggled for independence from the greater ones. This gave rise to a new sense of national identity. In music, composers began looking to the traditions, myths and legends of their own countries for musical ideas.

1 Russia

In St Petersburg*, five composers met to look for Russian stories for their operas and symphonic poems. The group—Balkirev, Mussorgsky, Borodin, Rimsky-Korsakov and Cui—were known as the "Mighty Handful".

2

Rachmaninov composed music in the Romantic style. He left Russia soon after the Revolution and finally settled in the U.S.A., but remained deeply attached to his homeland. He was also a very great pianist.

Folk-song and folk-dance

When composers started wanting to create national styles, they began to take an interest in folk music—unwritten music found mainly in country areas.

Czechoslovakia

Smetana and Dvořák both worked to set up a Czech national style of music, making use of Czech legends, folk songs and dances. Here is a scene from Smetana's opera *The Bartered Bride*.

Hungary

In the 20th century, Zoltán Kodály toured Hungary collecting folk songs that would otherwise have died out. He and Bartók used the rhythms and tunes as a basis for many of their works.

Finland

Finland had hardly produced any composers at all, until Jean Sibelius. He wrote seven symphonies which perfectly captured the feeling of his country's bleak lakes and forests.

Norway

In Norway, Edvard Grieg, wrote about the mountains and fjords. One of his best known works is the music he wrote for *Peer Gynt*, the play by his friend, Henrik Ibsen.

*St Petersburg is now called Leningrad.

1 England

In England, Ralph Vaughan Williams and Gustave Holst went on walking tours in the countryside, often noting down old local songs. England had had very few notable composers for almost 100 years and they became the centre of a great revival of English music. They were particularly interested in the music of the great Tudor Age.

France

In France, music developed together with the Impressionist movement in painting. Debussy and Ravel were the main composers. Above is a programme design for Debussy's ballet *L'Après-Midi D'Un Faune.*

Edward Elgar was the first important figure in this revival of English music. The success of his *Enigma Variations,* which was performed all over the world, gave new confidence to other English composers.

Frederick Delius is best known for his descriptive orchestral pieces, such as *Brigg Fair,* based on a Lincolnshire folk song. He spent most of his life abroad. Here he is at his home at Grez-sur-Loing, France.

America

Dvořák helped Americans to look to their own past, particularly their negro heritage, for musical inspiration. Charles Ives and later George Gershwin also showed how it could be used in classical music.

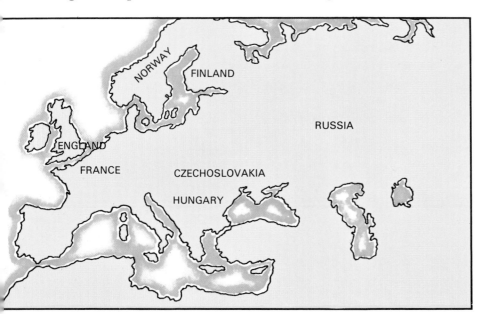

Music to listen to

Rimsky-Korsakov (AD1844/1908)
Scheherazade (symphonic poem)

Mussorgsky (AD1839/1881)
Pictures at an Exhibition (suite)
Nursery Songs

Rachmaninov (AD1873/1943)
Piano Concerto No. 2

Dvořák (AD1841/1934)
Symphony No. 9, "The New World"
Serenade in E for strings

Elgar (AD1857/1934)
Pomp and Circumstances Marches 1–5
Symphony No. 1 in A flat

Vaughan Williams (AD1872/1958)
Greensleeves Fantasia

Operetta and Musicals

Operetta is similar to opera, except that the stories are always amusing. The tunes are catchier and most of the words are spoken rather than sung. It became popular in the Western World from about 1850 onwards.

The musical has developed in the 20th century from a combination of operetta and Music Hall.

In Paris, Jules Offenbach put this high-kicking dance called the can-can, in his operetta, *Orpheus in the Underworld.* The dance was very popular, but some people were shocked.

In England, the writer, Gilbert, and the composer, Sullivan, used operetta to make fun of opera and society. This scene is from *Iolanthe,* where they mock the House of Lords.

The Merry Widow by Fran[z] Lehár is typical of the mo[re] romantic operettas of Vienna. It was this tradition that influenced the American musicals of the 1930s and 1940s.

Kurt Weill based *The Threepenny Opera* (1928) on music played in nightclubs. He used actors who could sing, rather than singers, and this became one of the main differences between musicals and operettas.

Music played an important part in the early cinema. The first talking picture, *The Jazz Singer* (1927), was a musical, as were many of the films that followed it. The stories were romantic fantasies, or comments on events of the time. They often included dancing too. Among the most spectacular were the musicals made by the dance director, Busby Berkeley. This scene is from his musical, *The Ziegfeld Girl.*

By World War II, musicals with present day themes became more popular. *Oklahoma!,* a story set in the American countryside, opened in 1943. It ran in New York for five years, with 2,212 performances.

Dance became even more important in musicals such as *West Side Story* (1957). It was a bit like an opera, as the story was tragic, and the music was composed by the classical musician, Leonard Bernstein.

The 1970s saw the arrival of the rock opera—rock music with a story. The first was *Tommy* by The Who. Several others followed. *Jesus Christ Superstar* (above) is probably the most successful.

Jazz

Jazz is a kind of music that developed in America in the last years of the 19th century. The music is not usually written down but is "improvised" by the players. This means that the players start with a musical idea and extend and develop it as they go along.

It has had a great influence on both classical and pop music and lies somewhere between the two. It was at its most popular in the 1930s and 1940s.

Jazz can be traced back to the songs sung by the black slaves, who had been brought over from Africa to work on the plantations in the southern states of the U.S.A., in the 19th century.

In 1866 slavery was abolished and many ex-slaves moved to southern cities, like New Orleans. There they formed their own town bands, which played marches and dances in the streets, especially for funerals.

These musicians also started playing in the bars of New Orleans. Their bands usually included a rhythm section (a string bass, guitar, banjo or piano) as well as brass instruments.

One early type of jazz is called ragtime and is usually played on the piano. Here is the cover of one of the rags written by the pianist and composer, Scott Joplin.

The "Jazz Age" really began after World War I. In the 1920s radio, records and films helped to make it internationally popular, and Chicago became its new centre. In the 1930s and 1940s the best players went to New York and Big Bands and Swing Bands (above), with band leaders like Duke Ellington, Count Basie and Benny Goodman, became all the rage.

Louis Armstrong

Because jazz is usually improvised music, players are really more important than composers. The trumpeter Louis Armstrong was one of the greatest of all jazz musicians.

Duke Ellington

Duke Ellington was a pianist and band leader. Unlike most jazz composers, he wrote his compositions down, but he managed to keep the feeling that it was improvised.

Saxophones

Mouthpiece with reed like a woodwind instrument.

Metal tube, like a brass instrument.

The saxophone was invented by a Belgian instrument maker, called Adolphe Sax, in about 1840. It was adopted by early jazz musicians and became one of the most important ingredients in jazz bands.

Popular Music

In the Western world a lighter kind of music has always existed alongside the more serious classical music. This kind of music is much more closely related to everyday life than classical music, and is called "popular" music, which means "music of the people". It includes folk-songs and dances, traditional ballads, work songs and all the different types of music that have become known as "pop".

Folk-songs

Many folk-songs and folk-dances originally celebrated a particular festival or time of year, like May Day, Christmas or the coming of spring. No-one knows when most of them were composed.

Work-songs

Sea shanties, railway songs and negro work-songs were all made up by people who did heavy work. They used strong rhythms, and often had one part for the gang leader and a chorus for the rest of the gang.

Music Hall

During the 19th century, many people moved to the cities in search of work. The owners of the bars where they went to drink started employing singers and entertainers. Soon, special theatres called Music Halls were built for this kind of entertainment, which also became known as "variety" or "vaudeville". Songs sung in Music Halls were the big hits of the day.

Radio broadcasting

Radio broadcasting began in the 1920s. Songwriters and singers now had the opportunity of getting their songs heard by much larger audiences and of becoming very famous. One of the most successful of the early radio stars was the singer, Bing Crosby.

Gramophones and records

In the 1920s gramophones and records became widely available and people started to have them in their homes. The records were made of a substance called shellac, which broke very easily. They played at a speed of 78 revolutions per minute, each side lasting about four minutes. The first really popular ones were of dance music, like the charleston.

1 Pop music

In the 1950s, rock n' roll became wildly popular with young people all over America and later in Europe. Elvis Presley was the most successful of a series of rock n' roll solo singers.

In the early 1960s pop music in England began to be played by "groups", usually consisting of lead, rhythm and bass guitarists and a drummer. The Beatles were the first group to become world-famous.

1 New inventions

Long playing records (LPs) and singles, made of unbreakable plastic, appeared in the 1950s, followed in the 1960s by stereo recordings, which create a sound much closer to that of live music.

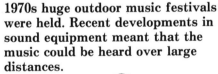

Pop music was spread to huge audiences by television, film, radio and records. This meant that live performances also attracted large audiences. In the late 1960s and early

1970s huge outdoor music festivals were held. Recent developments in sound equipment meant that the music could be heard over large distances.

2

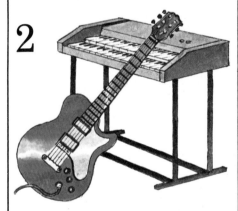

New instruments, like electric guitars, pianos and organs, have been developed and become widely used, and electronic instruments, like synthesizers*, can create totally new sounds.

4

Singers like Bob Dylan, used a mixture of folk-song and rock styles to write and sing "protest" songs. Their words are about the injustice they saw in the world around them.

5

In the 1970s various different styles of pop music came and went. One of these was disco music. With its strong and regular rhythm it brought in a new dancing craze.

3

The quality of sound from recordings of music has been vastly improved by the invention and development of tape recording. Modern recording studios are constantly getting new equipment.

See page 31

Classical Music in the 20th Century

The music of the 20th century includes a great variety of styles. Some composers have continued to use forms like the symphony and concerto, others have created new forms. Percussion instruments have become more important and electronic instruments have helped to create totally original sounds.

New directions

From the first years of the 20th century, composers began to break away from the system of music based on eight-note scales (keys), which had been used in Europe since the Renaissance. Very strict rules had developed for the key system and composers wanted something new.

1

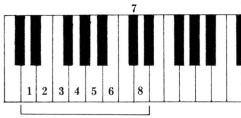

Eight-note scale (octave)

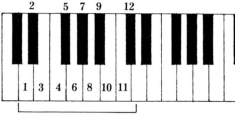

Twelve-note row

An Austrian composer called Arnold Schönberg developed a new system. He used a scale, or row, of 12 notes, using every note between the first and last note of the eight-note scale, instead of just some of them. Music composed using this system is called serial or atonal.

1

When the ballet, *The Rite of Spring,* by Igor Stravinsky, was first performed in Paris in 1913, it caused a riot. The people in the audience who hated it fought in the theatre with those who thought it was the most exciting music they had ever heard. The ballet is about a primitive Russian folk ritual for the beginning of spring and the music sometimes seems fierce and disturbing compared to earlier ballets.

The Rite of Spring was one of the ballets put on by Sergei Diaghilev (above). His Russian Ballet Company in Paris commissioned new works from many of the best composers, including Ravel and Debussy.

Igor Stravinsky was born in Russia, but also lived in France and America. During his life he wrote in several different styles and he had an immense influence over other composers. He died in 1971.

2

Composers have also experimented with new ways of writing music down, in order to express things that would be very difficult to express using the normal system.

New inventions

Some composers have experimented with new kinds of musical sound. Sometimes they use everyday noises like radios, door-keys or car horns.

Sometimes they alter traditional instruments, for example, by putting drawing pins and rubbers inside a piano, or playing a cymbal with a violin bow.

The invention of the tape recorder in the 1940s made it possible to create a vast new range of sounds by cutting tape, speeding it up, and playing it backwards. Often specially prepared tapes are now used in performance with live musicians.

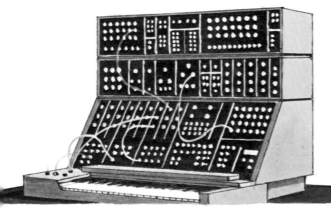

An even newer instrument, the synthesizer, uses a computer to imitate voices, instruments and other sounds. The computer can put them all together to make new sounds of its own.

Some composers of the 20th century

Dmitri Shostakovich wrote 15 symphonies and string quartets, which reflect his sadness at the terrible events happening in Russia in his time.

Olivier Messaien lives in France. He is most famous for his organ music and his piano works, which use the way birds sing as their basis.

Benjamin Britten lived on the coast in eastern England—the setting for his opera, *Peter Grimes.* He also wrote many works for boys choirs.

Witold Lutoslawski is one of Poland's greatest living composers. He uses both traditional musical ideas and modern serial techniques for his works.

Luciano Berio comes from Italy. He is one of the composers who has used electronic instruments and tape recordings in his compositions.

Peter Maxwell Davies is English but lives on one of the islands off the coast of Scotland. Often his music takes its theme from the islands' history.

Music to listen to

Schönberg (AD1874/1951)
Pierrot Lunaire
The Transfigured Night

Stravinsky (AD1882/1971)
The Firebird (ballet)
Pulcinella (ballet)
Symphony of Psalms

Messaien (born AD1908)
L'Ascension (for organ or orchestra)

Shostokovich (AD1906/1075)
Symphony No. 7, "The Leningrad"

Barber (born AD1910)
Adagio for Strings
Essay for Orchestra

Britten (AD1913/1976)
Young Person's Guide to the Orchestra
Ceremony of Carols

Lutoslawski (born AD1913)
Concerto for Orchestra
Les Espaces de Sommeil

Berio (born AD1925)
Sequenza 1 to 9

Maxwell Davies (born AD1934)
The Two Fiddlers (opera)
The Martyrdom of
St Magnus (opera)

Index